I0476787

How to Write an Easy Read.

by Lynette Clarke

ABOUT THE AUTHOR

Maybe you have been asked to complete this guide as part of your workplace training. Perhaps it was on your course reading list. Then again, you might have just spotted this and thought you'd give it a try. Either way, by the time you finish this guide, you will have mastered something that will serve you well.

Hello, I'm Lyn Clarke and inside are insights that I've acquired from more than 30 years of writing for a living.

Since the '80s I have worked as a writer on ad campaigns. I've honed my skills, writing for all sectors across many formats. What is more, I've learned from decades of practice what works and what doesn't.

Throughout my career, much of what I write has been measured. Either through increased market share. Or by the volume of people who send in a coupon, call a phone number or visit a web site.

My words have helped to sell billions of dollars in products, while raising many millions for Not For Profits. People read what I write and they act upon it. In fact, I am proud to say that my campaigns not only meet but often exceed the sales' targets and response rates.

I first thought about writing this guide after working with my uni students. When I shared my insights, I noticed each student's writing improved. But why stop there?

In recent times I have also been employed by firms to help their staff to write simply and clearly.

As most people soon find out - an easy read is one of the hardest things you can write. It takes real effort to present your thoughts in a reader-friendly way.

So to help you, I have now compiled all these writing tips along with set tasks. They're here, in this one, step-by-step guide for you to work through.

You can complete this guide, doing chapters as you please. Or you can set aside time for the purpose. To go from start to finish, best allow two and a half days. That is four lessons daily.

When next you have a message to get across, just apply the learnings that are covered inside. This way you can start writing simply, clearly and for your readers always.

Further to this guide, I also work in person with firms and other groups. My workshops, on your site, will help to take your people through the process and answer their questions on the spot.

If you wish to discuss having a workshop, please contact me on <u>www.howtowriteaneasyread.com.au</u>.

INDEX

CHAPTERS	PAGE

LET'S START HERE

No matter what you write, read this first.

"Think like a wise man but communicate in the language of the people." William Butler Yeats. Irish poet and playwright. 1865-1939.

Want to seem even smarter than you do now?

How about more honest?

Soon others could find that they like you a lot. Or start thinking of you as a friend.

It's true. That's the power of writing an easy read but these pluses will be covered later, along with others.

The concept is not new. From Churchill to Einstein, many of those famous in their fields have long praised the merits of simple writing. Some have even released books on the subject.

Even so, this guide is unlike any other because, to be of any lasting value, it needed to delve further.

Inside, as you would expect, you will find tips on writing simply and clearly. Still, this is just part of the process.

Each chapter also tackles those myths about writing that we have just come to accept without question.

You see the problem is that we have been programmed to write in a complex way.

At school we are urged to write long-winded essays and to use big words. Our marks often depend on it. It can be the same at uni. Even after we secure a job, we'll keep churning this stuff out.

Why? Because after a lifetime of being forced to use lengthy words and verbose phrasing, it has become second nature.

Sure it makes sense to write simply. So if you explain this to someone, they are bound to follow your advice. But for how long?

As soon as a memo needs to go out quickly, they'll just revert back to old ways. After all, it's what we know. We can do it without thinking. Hence the need to look at our bad writing habits and break them once and for all.

First though, before we begin, I need to be very clear with you about something.

This guide is not about content.
Instead it deals with technique.

Some people have asked me why I didn't call this book "How to be a better writer". But that would have been something else, aimed at would-be authors.

Instead this is a book for all people and the many kinds of writing we need to do in our lives.

Most of us write often. On a daily basis we may compose emails, letters, memos and so much more. Still practice doesn't always make perfect.

Years ago I taught myself to type. I type every day. I'm very fast but I make many errors. The same could be said for most people's writing.

**Today much of what is written
goes over our heads.**

If you have ever installed something you will know that most "How to" guides are not easy-to-follow.

The same can be said for contracts. Here there needs to be pages of small print just to cover off those legal terms. These are just the start.

In each head office you'll find uni grads. Trouble is that they often need to write memos to workers in the plant, the warehouse or the store. So we have staff with degrees writing to workers who did not finish high school. Or writing to those who have English as a second language.

If the execs don't write clearly and simply, the workers could be confused or, worse still, just ignore the memo. Let's hope the message is not about some vital health and safety issue.

As I looked, I found more demand for writing to be simple. Even in terms of cost control.

Each day queries are handled by call centres because what was written did not make sense. A brochure, a letter, the terms of something or other. It doesn't matter what piece it is. The fact is, if something is not clear it can end up costing in lost sales and staff time, among others. And it doesn't stop there.

With so much being done via smart phones and laptops, most jobs involve some kind of writing. Just think about how many emails a staff member may send on any day.

The need has become even greater with the growth of the web and the influx of online forums. These days many roles call for staff to write content for sites, blogs and Facebook.

In these social contexts it has become all the more crucial to write in a reader-friendly way.

So why does there need to be a guide? Isn't it easy to write simply?

Well you would think it should be easy but it isn't. Not at all. In truth, working your way through this guide will be a real challenge at times. Even so, the outcome will be worth it.

With each page you will find your writing improves. Your choice of words will become simpler and your message clearer. Better still, your writing will become easy to read.

Ready? Then let's start.

Inside you will find chapters (or lessons) to be done in order.

You must read each lesson from start to finish.

Take your time and even read out loud if you can.

Then complete the set tasks for that section.

Do not skip any lessons.

Do not jump ahead to complete tasks.

To get the most value from this book, you must work through the process as it has been set out.

This book can be used by staff in all fields to make comms clearer in the workplace. It can also assist with all manner of speeches, statements, terms, brochures, scripts, guides, letters and the like.

No matter what you write, this book will help to make it clearer and easy to read. In fact, after working your way through this book you will never again bash out long-winded, complex waffle. Instead you will write to get your message across.

LESSON 1

Forget what you've been taught.

"The shorter and the plainer the better."
Beatrix Potter. English author and illustrator.
1866-1943.

If you have ever gone out of your way to find a bigger word to impress your reader, you're not alone. It seems that from the day we pick up our first pencil, we are urged to use long words. Also to over-write.

How often has a mark called for a word count to be met? Write 5,000 words on "How to bore readers senseless".

Now don't get me wrong.
This is not about dumbing down content.

Instead it's about writing in a concise and clear way so people will know what you mean.

For instance, if I were to ask you how to get to Point B, you would give me the most direct route. You would not have me travel out of my way along extra roads, streets and highways, just for the sake of it. Why would you? That would only be a waste of your time and mine.

It's the same for much of what you write. Don't take your readers on a detour by choosing words they may need to look up. Instead opt for the very simplest, clearest and quickest approach always.

It's a fact that the more skilled someone is, the simpler they make it seem.

People who are the very best at what they do always make it look easy.

Ever watched a chef prepare a meal on a cooking programme? It all looks so straight forward you are sure you could do that too. Until of course you try. It's the same with a writer.

So don't kid yourself that filling your writing with long words and verbose statements will make you look smart. The truth is that your readers have more than likely switched off. They're not thinking about how smart you are. Their thoughts are now somewhere else.

Still, you're not to blame for thinking that you need to write this way to impress. You've been told this time and again.

For as long as most of us can recall, we have been taught that the bigger the word the better. We have even been led to believe that complex writing is clever, while clearer writing is less so. Really, though, it's the other way around.

The fact is this. It takes far more skill and much greater effort to convey yourself simply.

Perhaps, like most people, you have sometimes hoped that using big words would make your message seem more profound. Or that your grasp of the English language would cover a lack of subject matter. Of course the trouble here is that readers can see through this.

When I first told my students to use shorter words, they argued that these would make them look stupid.

They didn't get that it's the content that shows off your smarts, not the words you choose to use.

Simple writing just ensures that people will read what you write and get the point you are making. Surely, there is nothing stupid in that. In fact, it's a whole lot smarter than setting out to write something that could confuse the reader.

Don't forget! If you are writing something that must be read, followed or actioned then people need to get what you're saying. So let's not waste any words on writing that will be put to one side and never picked up again.

You are about to do the set tasks for Lesson 1.

There is no rush here. This is not about speed. Instead, feel free to work on these tasks at your own pace, giving yourself plenty of time.

Like most people, you may think that writing simply will be both quick and easy. The truth is, it's neither.

These tasks will challenge you.

There will be times when you will struggle. You may even be tempted to give up. Please don't though.

It has been drummed into us to use big words and long-winded phrasing. So much so, we now do it without thinking. But what good is that if your readers are not getting the message you are trying to make? Or not liking the way your message reads.

By working through these ten lessons, you will at last know "How to write an easy read". And no matter what you write, that's a really good skill to have.

The best way to write simply is to only use words of one and two syllables (or vowel sounds).

The one/two approach.

TASK 1A. Replace "employment" with words of one/two syllables. For instance: Em-ploy-ment is three so it's out. Work is one so it's in. There is no limit to the number of words you can use. But they must all be one or two syllables.

1. Work

2. Earning an income

3. How you make a living

4. _____

5. _____

6. _____

7. _____

8. _____

9. _____

10. _____
(Some answers listed at the back of this book)

With practice, finding simpler words will become second nature.

Some words of two syllables (or vowel sounds) may seem like big words but you can say them quickly. Speed implies ease.

TASK 1B. Replace "education" with word/s of one or two syllables. There is no limit to the number of words you can use. But they must all be one or two syllables.

1. Schooling

2. Formal learning

3. _____

4. _____

5. _____

6. _____

7. _____

8. _____

9. _____

10._____

(Some answers listed at the back of this book)

You're getting better at this, aren't you?

If you have English as a second language, you could struggle with a word like "malfunctioned". "Stopped working" is a much better choice. When you stick to using words of one or two syllables (vowel sounds), people get what you're saying.

TASK 1C. Replace "malfunctioned". There is no limit to the number of words you can use. But they must all be one or two syllables.

1. Stopped working

2. _____

3. _____

4. _____

5. _____

6. _____

7. _____

8. _____

9. _____

10. _____

(Some answers listed at the back of this book)

Keep doing this and you will get faster.

If there is a risk that your readers might not know the meaning of a word, use something else. Don't forget that writing a few words your readers will know is better than one word they don't.

TASK 1D. Replace "obsolete" with word/s of one/ two syllables.

1. Old fashioned

2. _____

3. _____

4. _____

5. _____

6. _____

7. _____

8. _____

9. _____

10._____

(Some answers listed at the back of this book)

In time you will do this without thinking.

If you keep looking for a simpler way to say something, it will become the norm. It takes practice to break old habits though. So how about one more for good measure?

TASK 1E. Replace "abbreviate" with word/s of one/ two syllables. There is no limit to the number of words you can use.

1. Cut down

2. _____

3. _____

4. _____

5. _____

6. _____

7. _____

8. _____

9. _____

10._____

(Some answers listed at the back of this book)

LESSON 2

Complex writing does nothing for you.

"Have something to say, and say it as clearly as you can. That is the only secret of style."
Matthew Arnold. British author/cultural critic.
1822 -1888.

Not long back I was reading about Daniel M. Oppenheimer. He is an associate professor of psychology at Princeton University. In 2006 he won an Ig Nobel Award in literature from Harvard.

The prize was for Oppenheimer's paper "Consequences of Erudite Vernacular Utilized Irrespective of Necessity: Problems with using long words needlessly"[i]. Don't you just love his paper's title? The complex versus the simple right there in front of your eyes.

Anyway, his paper appealed to me because it confirmed what I know to be true.

For his study into the use of language, Oppenheimer showed students essays by many writers.

The students were told that these writers were all vying for a place in grad school. The students were then asked to read and rate this work, picking those they thought were the smartest.

In some cases, the essays had been altered prior to the study, changing smaller words for longer, more complex ones. But none of the students who were reading the essays knew this. Instead they just read all essays and rated them as they had been asked.

So did using long words make any of these writers appear to be smarter? Or did those writers whose essays were changed to have complex words secure the most places? Not at all.

In fact, the results from this study showed the simpler the essays, the more clever the writers were deemed to be.

So how does using simple language make you seem smarter?

Some of my students have asked this question over the years. This is what I tell them.

Simple writing says you know a lot. If you need big words to impress, maybe the real problem is your lack of subject matter. Using simpler words says your content can support itself. Believe me, the reader knows a fake when they see one.

Simple writing ensures your message makes sense. When you use easy-to-follow language the message is clearer. So those who write this way appear to be more skilled in putting forward their point of view.

Simpler writing also aids recall. Reading a whole lot of complex, long-winded text is boring. Readers just switch off. The writing confuses. It seems pointless. A waste of time. A waste of space. Something you will forget as soon as you stop reading if not before.

So your use of big words makes you look stupid, a fake and a waste of space. If these are not enough, there are even more reasons to write simply and clearly.

Complex writing is like a bad joke. If you don't get a joke, do you like it? Would not getting someone's joke make you prefer that comic over other ones? Would you repeat a joke if its punch line made no sense? No, not at all.

You'd just put that bad joke out of your mind, never to think of it again. It's the same with writing.

Your writing can make people like you more, less or not at all.

When you write complex content, some readers will blame themselves for not getting the point. Others will blame you for not making yourself clearer. Then there'll be those who'll simply stop reading because it's just too hard.

So here's the question. Are you writing in a complex way to make readers feel bad or just bored?

You've heard the saying "reading between the lines"? Then think about this. When you use words your readers don't know they may just come up with a couple of meanings of their own. Like "pompous", "show off", "try hard". So in an effort to impress you've become someone to ignore or dislike.

Sure there will be times when you can write the most complex papers - when your readers will demand this. This could apply to a boss, a colleague, a peer or someone with whom you share knowledge on a certain subject.

Even so, for the most part, if you want readers to be engaged rather than repelled, stick to writing simply.

The one/two approach.

TASK 2A. Replace "calculations" with words of one or two syllables. There is no limit to the number of words you can use.

1. The math

2. Number crunching

3. Figures

4. _____

5. _____

6. _____

7. _____

8. _____

9. _____

10._____

(Some answers listed at the back of this book)

The one/two approach in context.

Now using the words you came up with before, see which ones can replace "calculations" in each sentence below. Then rewrite it. For this task you are only looking at changing one word. The one that has a line under it. Do not alter or remove any others.

TASK 2B.
As part of the tender we did the <u>calculations</u>.

_____

_____

TASK 2C.
Some <u>calculations</u> were needed for the pitch.

_____

_____

TASK 2D.
Show us how you came to those <u>calculations.</u>

_____

_____

As you can see above, when you change a word in context, your choices are fewer. Even so, it is worth the effort to find a clearer way to write something.

There is no limit to how many words you use. But all the words must be one or two syllables.

The one/two approach.

TASK 2E. Replace "depreciation" with words of one or two syllables (vowel sounds).

1. Reduced value since purchase

2. Falling in value over time

3. _____

4. _____

5. _____

6. _____

7. _____

8. _____

9. _____

10._____

(Some answers listed at the back of this book)

The one/two approach in context.

Now using the words you came up with before, see which ones can replace "depreciation" in each sentence below. You are only looking at changing that one word.

TASK 2F.
Include each car's <u>depreciation</u> in your audit.

_____

_____

TASK 2G.
Highlight all items that are at risk of <u>depreciation</u>.

_____

_____

TASK 2H.
Be sure to claim any machine <u>depreciation</u>.

_____

_____

As you can see above, when you change a word in context, your choices are fewer. Even so, it is worth the effort to find a clearer way to write something.

If your reader may need to look up a word, change it.

The one/two approach.

TASK 2I. Replace "dissension" with words of one or two syllables. There is no limit to the number of words you can use.

1. Rifts

2. _____

3. _____

4. _____

5. _____

6. _____

7. _____

8. _____

9. _____

10._____

(Some answers listed at the back of this book)

The one/two approach in context.

Now using the words you came up with before, see which ones can replace "dissension" in each sentence below. Don't forget, you are only looking at changing that one word.

TASK 2J.
<u>Dissension</u> threatens output.

_____

_____

TASK 2K.
We must nip any <u>dissension</u> in the bud.

_____

_____

TASK 2L.
There have been reports of <u>dissension.</u>

_____

_____

As you can see above, when you change a word in context, your choices are fewer. Even so, it is worth the effort to find a clearer way to write something.

LESSON 3

Write to include and engage.

**"Speak properly, and in as few words as you can,
but always plainly; for the end of speech is not
ostentation, but to be understood."
William Penn. English philosopher. 1644-1718.**

Okay you want your writing to reflect well on you. Even so, is it really about making you look good? If you are writing to staff, clients, prospects or even the public, surely you want much more from your words.

Your choice of words can make the reader like you a lot, or less so. It can also decide if a shopper prefers your brand. Further to these, the way you write may even affect how your readers feel about themselves. It's true.

There is power in words so be careful not to abuse it.

Think back to the school playground and how kids would whisper to each other. Often they'd do this in front of a youngster to make him or her feel left out.

It's not nice. It's what bullies do. Are you any better, though, if you write in a way that excludes some of your readers?

When you put pen to paper or tap away at the keyboard, think of that whisper in the playground. Then decide to write in a way that welcomes and includes your readers.

It will reflect well on you if you do.

You see, when we get what we are reading, there is a shared common ground between the writer and us.

So the way you write can make you seem like someone the reader knows and likes. If the reader is a staff member, client or prospect, then surely this rapport is just what you'd want. All the more reason to write simply.

Write for the reader always.

It seems like common sense but it's not a given. Many times I have seen ads written to please the client rather than appeal to the target market.

It doesn't stop there.

Admin staff often need to write memos to workers at the plant who have English as a second language. Trouble is these admin people may write to impress the boss who will see the memo before it goes out.

If you ever find yourself tempted to do this, just show the boss your memo and no one else. After all, this memo will now be unclear to those who really need to read it.

Many firms these days have this divide, where one section is out of sync with the others.

What is more, this divide can damage staff morale.

When you send out memos that use complex words, some workers will feel out of their depth. Even worse, it may seem like you are speaking over these people's heads on purpose.

In fact, workers could think that the memo they can't read is not for them at all. Instead, the jargon heavy message with its big words must be for the guys in head office.

So, at the very least, make sure that what you write brings people closer, rather than pushes them further apart.

When I suggest writing simply, there are always those who feel that their freedom of speech is somehow being threatened. These people want their grasp of the English language to be used in full.

Perhaps you feel like this also. Then let me just say this. There will always be times when you can write just as you prefer. When your readers will not only be impressed but expect you to write that way. This could apply if you were writing to a peer with whom you share knowledge about a certain subject.

For the most part though, writing simply and clearly is the way to go.

Remove the guess work and your readers will be grateful.

If someone were not fluent in English, would you prefer they just speak in their mother tongue? Surely not. Why would you? Even if you caught the odd word, for the most part you'd have no idea what they're saying.

Instead, wouldn't you just prefer the person spoke with what little English they had? It might be a simpler message and more to the point but at least you would get the gist.

When you use words that your readers don't know it is like you are speaking to them in a foreign language. You are putting the onus on them to make sense of these strange words, to try and guess what you mean. You are making reading hard work and for what reason?

It is just pointless to try and confuse your readers. It doesn't serve you. It doesn't serve them. It just defeats the purpose of writing in the first place, doesn't it?

So if you want people to read what you've written and get the meaning, opt for plain English always.

**Don't forget.
Writing simply is not about talking down.**

Some people may argue that when you write simply you are speaking down to readers? Not so.

After all, writing simply is about making sure that the message gets across. It does not dictate the message.

For instance, I could tell you: "Brush your hair or it will become knotted". If I wrote something like this, of course, you may think I am talking down to you and rightly so.

Then again I could say: "Brush your hair, starting at the ends and slowly working your way up. This way any knotted clumps will slide through each strand and your hair will not split". This time, you would not think I was talking down to you. Why? Because the message has more depth to it. It's a better message.

You only have to read the quotes throughout this guide from the likes of Churchill. No one would question that these people I've quoted are among the smartest our world has known. Yet these great minds are also big fans of saying things simply.

Your smarts are never conveyed by the words you choose, but rather the nature of your content.

Remind yourself of this each time you write.

Are you breaking those old habits? Let's see.

Quick word changes.

TASK 3. In each sentence replace the word that has a line under it. Don't forget you can replace one word with more. Just so long as they are all one or two syllables.

Sample:
We need eight seats at the very <u>minimum</u>.
Changed to:
We need eight seats at the very <u>least</u>.

A. The client expressed her <u>appreciation</u>.

_____

B. It's a fully <u>operational</u> facility.

_____

C. All <u>questionnaires</u> have been finished.

_____

D. He <u>persevered</u> with the plans.

_____

E. The cost is for each <u>individual</u>.

_____

F. It proved to be an <u>effortless</u> task completed well before time.

_____

G. A virus has <u>infiltrated</u> the system.

_____

H. Each of these staff will need to work <u>independently</u>.

_____

I. This <u>represents</u> all members.

_____

J. You will need to hand in your <u>resignation.</u>

_____

K. Every intern has <u>difficulties</u> with the systems.

_____

L. We need you to <u>illuminate</u> the issues.

_____

M. He fills in <u>occasionally.</u>

_____

N. Spread the mixture <u>liberally.</u>

_____

O. The <u>activity</u> calls for your input.

_____

P. Please secure <u>accommodation.</u>

_____

Q. We are looking for someone who is known for <u>frugality.</u>

_____

R. All rules should be <u>uniform</u> across the firm.

_____

S. One entry was <u>superior.</u>

_____

T. This staff member is under <u>surveillance.</u>

_____

U. These are all <u>necessities</u>.

_____

V. <u>Newspaper</u> reports support the firm's forecasts.

_____

W. <u>Demonstrate</u> the new unit.

_____

X. The area has been <u>stabilised</u>.

_____

Y. The union called for <u>industrial</u> action.

_____

Z. Please <u>estimate</u> the costs.

_____

(Some answers listed at the back of this book)

LESSON 4

Short words add value.

"Broadly speaking, the short words are the best, and the old words when short are best of all." Winston Churchill. The only British PM awarded a Nobel Prize in Literature. 1874-1965.

Think back to the biggest moments in your life. The very times that will flash before your eyes when you take your last breath.

Happy birthday.

Make a wish.

Blow out the candles.

I got my licence.

Want to go out?

I'd like to see more of you.

Can I kiss you?

You've passed.

Well done!

I love you.

You've got the job.

Will you marry me?

We're engaged.

All the best.

I now pronounce you man and wife.

Have a safe trip.

We've found the house of our dreams.

It's going to be auctioned

Any more bids.

Sold.

Sign on the dotted line.

We're having a baby.

It's a boy.

It's a girl.

You've got the job. When can you start?

I would like a pay rise.

You've been seeing someone else?

I want a divorce.

I want you back.

It's too late for all that.

I've met someone else.

Good for you.

It's time for that golden hand shake.

Speech!

We need to down size.

A sea change.

A tree change.

Maybe even become grey nomads.

Apply for our passports.

Take a cruise.

The trip of a lifetime.

Don't forget to write.

Pick up some duty free.

It's good to be back home.

What's this?

I've found a lump.

I'm in pain.

A bit dizzy, breathless, sweaty.

We'll take some blood.

Run some tests.

It's not good news, I'm afraid.

You need to sort out your affairs.

Can I give you your last rites?

From ashes to ashes, dust to dust.

Rest in peace.

It's true isn't it? Those big events, the ones that can change your life tend to be conveyed with a few short words. We get it. There is no need to labour the point.

Instead we get married and we say: "I do" or "I will".

We bring a new life into the world and the doctor tells us: "It's a boy" or "It's a girl".

We fall out of love and we say: "It's over". Or "I want a divorce".

We lose a loved one and to break the news to others, they have "died". They have "gone". They have "passed".

**The bigger the event the simpler the words
we choose to convey it.**

For instance: "That's one small step for a man, one giant leap for mankind". In July 1969, could Neil Armstrong have summed up man's first walk on the moon any better? Would using big words have given this moment more weight? I doubt it.

You've heard the saying "words are not enough". I also like to think that often words need not be more. They should just state things the way they are, rather than detract from the message.

Sure there may be times when bigger, complex words have been used for major events. Even so, if this were a must, surely they'd be used all the time.

Don't forget that when you use simple words, you are letting the focus rest squarely on what you are writing about. You are saying this here is what matters and not the words you are using to describe it.

By choosing simple, clear words you add value to your subject, product or service.

You are saying your message is strong enough, it doesn't need to be dressed up.

Using simple words is all about the content and isn't that why you are writing in the first place?

Why say "my apologies" when you can say "sorry"?

Australia's Aboriginals had long wanted the powers that be to address the wrongs that had been done by the white settlers.

The wrongs covered tribes being slaughtered. Also children being taken from their parents. In all, some of the most shocking crimes and heart wrenching deeds. Yet for all these, my country's native people just wanted to hear one word and that was "sorry".

Never think for a moment that small words don't carry weight or they lack strength. It's simply not true.

More often than not it's the smallest words that have the greatest impact.

On February 13, 2008 the PM Kevin Rudd gave the speech our nation had waited years to hear. At first, the working title for the address was "Prime Minister Kevin Rudd - Apology to Australia's Indigenous People". Later it was condensed to "Rudd's sorry speech".

There's a lesson in this alone.

Right throughout Australia people stopped what they were doing to listen. The speech brought tears to my eyes and I was not alone there. That's how much power a simple word like "sorry" can have.

If we do not need big words at milestones like this, why do we need them in an office memo? An ad? A brochure? A guide? Or a letter, among other items?

The fact is, we don't.

Sometimes a word change can call for a rewrite.

Sentence changes.

TASK 4. In each sentence replace each lined word with those of one or two syllables (vowel sounds). As before, there is no limit to how many words you can use. This time, though, you may also need to rewrite the sentence to make the changes.

Sample:
The contract is <u>tentative</u> on meeting the schedule.
Changed to:
The contract will depend on meeting the schedule.

OR

Sample:
It's the tenant's <u>responsibility</u> to pay the rent on time.
Changed to:
It's up to the tenant to pay the rent on time.

OR

Sample:
Please complete the <u>documentation</u> then sign.
Changed to:
Please complete and sign the paper work.

Now your turn.

1.Once all the details are <u>finalised</u> we can proceed.

_____

_____

2. All entries must be <u>submitted</u> in writing.

_____

_____

3. It's <u>mandatory</u> for <u>employees</u> to clock in and out.

_____

_____

4. Admin has <u>instigated</u> a number of <u>modifications</u>.

_____

_____

5. Our <u>induction</u> program <u>introduces</u> staff to our <u>operations</u>.

_____

_____

6. <u>Following</u> is an <u>indication</u> of all your <u>investment</u> options.

_____

_____

7. As those topics are <u>peripheral,</u> we won't discuss them today.

_____

_____

8. It is <u>imperative</u> to <u>successfully</u> complete this <u>examination</u>.

_____

_____

9. Some <u>individuals experience difficulties</u> in <u>mastering</u> this.

_____

_____

10. There are a <u>plethora</u> of <u>opportunities</u> for <u>revenue</u> growth.

_____

_____

11. <u>Overbearing</u> workers can <u>exasperate</u> others on the team.

_____

_____

12. <u>Concentrate</u> when <u>operating</u> this <u>machinery</u>.

_____

_____

13. <u>Developed</u> <u>interpersonal</u> skills are <u>essential</u> in this <u>position</u>.

_____

_____

14. We seek an <u>intelligent</u>, <u>eloquent</u>, <u>effervescent</u> <u>candidate</u>.

_____

_____

15. Provide <u>facsimiles</u> of <u>documentation</u> with your <u>application</u>.

_____

_____

16. This would only happen in <u>extenuating</u> <u>circumstances</u>.

_____

_____

17. <u>Consider</u> this <u>carefully</u> before <u>answering</u> the question.

_____

_____

18. <u>Discussions</u> are <u>underway</u> between all <u>divisions</u>.

_____

_____

19. The <u>inventory</u> has been <u>itemised</u> and warehoused.

_____

_____

20. We are <u>anticipating</u> that it will have a <u>colloquial</u> feel.

_____

_____

21. <u>Collaboration</u> is <u>paramount</u> to this project.

_____

_____

22. It all comes down to your <u>perception</u> of recent events.

_____

_____

23. That person <u>demonstrated</u> an <u>overbearing</u> <u>demeanour</u>.

_____

_____

24. Become <u>familiarised</u> with the <u>legislation</u> then <u>implement</u>.

_____

_____

(Some answers listed at the back of this book)

LESSON 5
Simply said is best. Honest.

**"The finest words in the world are only vain
sounds if you can't understand them.
The best sentence? The shortest."
Anatole France. French poet, journalist, novelist.
1844-1924**

In Hamlet Act 3 Scene 2 the Queen says: "The lady protests too much, methinks"[ii]. This line by Shakespeare is often quoted. Very simply, it implies that the lady is not to be believed.

When he penned this line, Shakespeare was saying that those trying to deceive us will use more words. They'll go into greater detail. They will "protest too much". Why?

Perhaps they are trying to convince others. Maybe even themselves. Either way, saying more than the subject warrants can be a sign that someone is not to be trusted.

If you are choosing long words or over-writing, ask yourself this. Are you using big words and waffling to give your subject more credence? If you are, you're not alone. Lots of writers pad out their content.

Be warned though.

Readers can spot if you are saying a lot about very little. So if you want to be seen as honest and sincere, you'd be better off writing less and getting to the point.

Just look at those experts of spin – the people who govern us.

We elect those we believe and trust. Or, at the very least, believe and trust more than the others running. So it is worthwhile seeing how those on the hustings (or stump in the US) use language to sway voters.

It was Australia 1972. After 23 years of the Liberal-Country party, Labor came into power. The theme for the ALP's campaign was very simply "It's time"[iii].

Australia again. This time in the state of Victoria. In 1997 the Liberals won by a landslide after naming Labor "The guilty party"[iv].

Around the same time, Tony Blair ended 18 years of Tory rule in the UK. The term "New Labour" proved a hit with the people[v]. Also the belief that "Things can only get better"[vi].

In the USA in 2008, Barack Obama was voted into office by selling "Change we can believe in", "Change we need" and "Hope". This was followed by "Yes we can", a phrase that became his party's catch cry[vii].

In 2004 "Yes America can" had also been used by Bush with success[viii]. Prior to that, the line that secured Bush office in 2000 was just as succinct. Back then, the slogan "A new day" was followed by the chant "A new freedom".

Now this is not to say that themes alone win over voters. But it is worth noting that apart from proper nouns, most party lines are made up of words of one and two syllables.

For instance, a look at 38 winning US campaign slogans since 1900 comprised 176 words. Of these, only 14 words were three or more syllables and seven of these were the proper noun "America"[ix].

Simple language says you are being up-front.

This could explain why campaign slogans use basic language but it doesn't stop there. The use of simple words also extends into speeches.

Take the Gettysburg Address in 1863 in the midst of The American Civil War[x]. It may surprise you to know that this famous speech by US President Abraham Lincoln comprised only 267 words. Of these, 247 words were no more than one or two syllables. So over 92 per cent of this famous speech used simple language.

It's the same with Obama's address as the victor in the 2008 campaign[xi]. In it are 1,950 words of one and two syllables. That's compared to 144 words of three or more syllables.

If you remove proper nouns from the mix, one and two syllable words drop to 1,926. While three or more syllable words fall to 107. That's 18 smaller words for each one of three syllables or more. Or put simply, over 94 per cent of this address used one or two syllable words.

Even better, look at those lines that are still quoted today decades after they were first uttered.

"And so my fellow Americans ... ask not what your country can do for you ... ask what you can do for your country." J F Kennedy.

Apart from the proper noun "Americans", JFK kept this line to words of one and two syllables.

"I have a dream that one day this nation will rise up and live out the true meaning of its creed. We hold these truths to be self-evident, that all men are created equal." Martin Luther King.

It is worth noting that the only long words in this much quoted piece are "evident" and "created". Even so, would this sentence have lost its power if instead of "self-evident" Martin Luther King had used "clear"? Or if this great spokesman has opted for "made" rather than "created"?

"We shall fight on the beaches. We shall fight on the landing grounds. We shall fight in the fields and in the streets. We shall fight in the hills. We shall never surrender." Winston Churchill.

Here we have 32 smaller words for each one of three syllables or more. In fact, of the 33 words here, "surrender" is the only one that is three or more syllables.

Still, frank, no nonsense language is just what you'd expect from Churchill.

On June 18, 1940, a broadcast to all British subjects announced the fall of France to Germany[xii].

So how did Winston Churchill handle such a dire event? He used basic English, just as he'd always done.

In fact, Churchill spoke simply and clearly, starting his address with the sentence: "The news from France is very bad".

Some may argue that there are more one and two syllable words in the English language. Therefore short sounding words would be used more often. Perhaps but don't forget that we have been urged all our lives to use bigger words and to over-write.

From the moment we learn how to form letters we are taught that using big words and lengthy text is clever. We are told that our obscure words will impress. Our long-winded writing will persuade. We are brain washed to write more always with the belief that this will do wonders for our image.

Still, if big words and verbose text really carried all this power then the speech writers would exploit this. Surely they would write as much as they could and then some. Not so, though.

Instead those who craft speeches that win votes, rally support and report life changing events choose to go smaller and shorter. After all, getting into office and staying there requires that you are trusted and believed by your public.

Next time you are tempted to over-state something think of the lady who protests too much.

Don't forget that if you want your readers to take you at your word, then say it simply and clearly always.

**Don't pad your writing.
If a word isn't needed, get rid of it.**

Cut it out.

TASK 5. For each sentence below edit all words that are not needed. Then count how many words you have cut. As a guide 30 is okay, 60 is good but if manage to delete over 100 words - well done!

For instance:
To finish the project on time, please make sure that you stick to the schedule.

Cut to:
To finish the project on time, please stick to the schedule.

1. Really look at all your options.

_____

_____

_____

2. Be extra careful when using this unit near water.

_____

_____

_____

3. Only proceed with caution.

_____

_____

_____

4. They could use some helpful advice.

_____

_____

_____

5. Keep your watchful eye on the game.

_____

_____

_____

6. Take a good book with you.

_____

_____

_____

7. This will surely help to fill in some of the time.

_____

_____

_____

8. Ensure you always read before signing.

_____

_____

_____

9. With the right amount of training you could very well go the whole distance.

_____

_____

_____

10. Keep this safely secured under lock and key.

_____

_____

_____

11. Be careful, this sharp blade can cut you.

_____

_____

_____

12. Twelve times a year this machine has a monthly service.

_____

_____

_____

13. This road will take you all the way through to the river.

_____

_____

_____

14. Buy online and your goods will be dispatched to you the very same day.

_____

_____

_____

15. What is the total cost all up?

_____

_____

_____

16. Look at your many and varied options before you decide on the best one for you.

_____

_____

_____

17. In this field, study is very much part and parcel of the job.

_____

_____

_____

18. Rather than pretend, if you cannot follow the guidelines, ask and someone will help you with your query.

_____

_____

_____

19. Make a point to take a copy of all paperwork and keep this on file.

_____

_____

_____

20. You must complete the survey from start to finish before we can include your answers with the others.

_____

_____

_____

21. We have scheduled a meeting at head office 10am this Tuesday to discuss all the proposed changes at length.

_____

_____

_____

22. Guests will need to park in the basement under the building before taking the lift to the third floor.

_____

_____

_____

23. The faulty system can no longer be relied upon with constant breakdowns causing all kinds of delays.

_____

_____

_____

24. This sale item has been greatly reduced to 50 per cent so you can buy it for half price.

_____

_____

_____

25. You must check each single page, one after the other, then sign your name and date it.

_____

_____

_____

(Some answers listed at the back of this book)

LESSON 6
With simple language you create.

"Works of imagination should be written in very plain language; the more purely imaginative they are, the more necessary it is to be plain."
Samuel Taylor Coleridge. Poet/literary critic.
1772-1834.

It's true. As you will have learnt so far, it is not easy to say things simply. It goes against all we have been taught.

When you try to write using only words of one or two syllables, something happens. You have to really think about it. You have to play with what you have written. You have to sometimes change the entire sentence. So it stands to reason that the end result will be unique to you.

In other words, with simple writing you are less inclined to copy and more likely to create.

To explain my point, I grabbed two novels from my book shelf.

The first one I chose was "To Kill A Mockingbird" by Harper Lee. Then I turned to the first page[xiii]. On it I counted 298 words, of which only 13 are three syllables or more. When we factor in proper nouns though, the number of one/two syllable words is 280. At the same time, taking out proper nouns, the number of three or more syllable words drops to just 13. So over 95 per cent of words follow the one/two rule.

Next I reached for "The Catcher in the Rye" by J. D. Salinger[xiv]. On its first page are 344 words, of which only 18 are three syllables or more. Of course, when you take out proper nouns the number of one/two syllable words drops to 258, compared to just 13 with three or more. So yet again, as with the first novel, over 95 per cent of words follow the one/two rule.

Now I am not trying to convince you that two books could ever be called research. That would be an insult to you and me too.

Instead the point I am making is this.

If you can write a best seller mostly using words of one or two syllables, what does that say? It says here is a book using simple language that people want to read.

No surprise there really.

Now, if the same novel is then acclaimed by the critics as a classic, what does that show you? Well it shows that here is a book that, despite its simple language, is deemed to be writing at its best.

Now don't get me wrong. I am not saying that you cannot write a classic using big words and verbose text. Of course you can. Plenty of authors have done just that.

Instead what I am saying is that you don't need big words to write a classic. In fact, using basic language should in no way curtail the depth and breadth of brilliance that you can create. Just take the plays of William Shakespeare.

Of all the acclaimed works I have read, I believe Shakespeare's plays follow the one or two syllable rule most closely. To prove my point, I chose two of his plays at random. Then counted words of one and two syllables versus those of three or more. As with the novels I reviewed before, I used the first page for my findings.

I removed all proper nouns from act one, scene one of Shakespeare's play "The Tempest"[xv]. That left 102 words of one or two syllables, compared to just four of three or more. So what are the results? Over 96 per cent of words follow the one or two syllable rule.

I did the same with act one, scene one of Shakespeare's play "Romeo and Juliet"[xvi]. This time, when proper nouns are removed, it becomes 110:3. So in this case over 97 per cent of words comply with the one or two syllable rule.

And these findings are not only confined to novels.

Just listen to songs, read poems, even hire out some movies. The lyrics, the stanzas, those scripted gems we so love to quote are just short lines of simple words. Yet they seem like nothing else we have seen or heard before. That brings us to something else worth noting.

Simple writing aids recall.

When I write ad copy, I use basic language because it reads the way we speak. It comes across as sincere. And despite the effort it takes, it always sounds more "spur of the moment", rather than crafted.

This is even more so when I write DM letters, emails or I craft content for the web. But while I would like to take full credit for wisely choosing to write simply, sadly I cannot. In fact, basic language has been used to sell products and their merits for as long as ads have been produced. You only have to look at the award-winning copy of Bill Bernbach to see that straight talking rules.

Still, there is more to simple language that it helping us to sell. Simple language also seems to stay with us much longer.

On any given day you and I are exposed to hundreds, if not thousands, of ads. In fact, some sources claim the number can be as high as 3,000 if you count all contact points.

The question is, with this many logos fighting for space in your brain, how do brands stay top of mind?

In the last chapter we talked about party campaigns and the power of the slogan. Even so, people running for office were not the first to use the simple one liner to win over the public. It was ad land, among them the Mad Men themselves, who blazed that trail and with good reason.

Slogans work. They get into your head and remain there for weeks, months, years, even decades.

Often we are not even aware that a slogan has seeped into our grey matter until we shop. Then we find we prefer this brand over that one.

Sometimes we will even seek out a certain brand that we have never used before.

You may not be able to reel slogans off the top of your head. You don't need to. Plenty of focus groups have shown time and again that slogans are retained which, of course, begs the question.

What makes an ad slogan stay top of mind?

Some brands never change their slogans. Others alter as the product evolves or the market place changes. Either way some things remain the same.

In writing this chapter I looked at 320 ad slogans from around the world[xvii]. The slogans covered more than 200 brands, from many sectors and had been compiled over decades.

Here is what I found.

Taking out all proper nouns, like brands names, slogans tend to stick to simple words. In fact, of the 320 slogans, most of them (260) only used words of one and two syllables.

Not only were small words the norm, slogans tend to be succinct. In fact, of the 320 samples I reviewed, the mean is just five words per slogan.

Perhaps this is why ad slogans are easy to recall. Even so, staying top of mind is just part of the challenge.

Let's not forget that ads are all about taking what's unique about a product or service, then selling that one point. This could also explain why ad slogans tend to be short and simple. And herein lies another tip.

Along with simple words,
keep your message succinct.
Make just one point per sentence.

Throughout this book so far, I have talked about sticking to words of one or two syllables.

Even so, that is just half of it.

Have you ever reached the end of a sentence, to find you've lost track of how it began? This often happens when the sentence tries to cover off too many points.

Instead, to make your message succinct, keep each sentence to one statement.

It's what I call the "One Two, Two One approach". Mind you, I just call it this so you won't forget.

Firstly, it's one/two because that is how many syllables (vowel sounds) your words should have.

Then it's two one because 21 is the most number of words you should ever have in a sentence. By keeping each sentence to a word count, you can never say too much. It forces you to be single minded with each statement and make just one point.

Of course, this doesn't mean that you have to cut words. You could just make one long sentence into two shorter ones.

Lastly, add up one, two, two, one and you get six. Never have more than a six-sentenced paragraph (or block of text).

Here's why the "One Two, Two One Approach" works:

- At the very least, your writing should make sense. By using short words of one and two syllables, there is greater chance that your reader can grasp what you're saying.

- Your writing must look like a quick read and by keeping each sentence to 21 words or less it will.

After all your choice of words won't matter if those long lines and big blocks of text put your readers off.

Don't forget, that no matter what you write, speed implies ease and vice versa.

If something seems quick, we perceive it to be easy. If something is easy, we perceive it to be quick.

This theory applies to most things in life and that includes the way you write.

A sentence should have no more than 21 words.

Turn commas into full stops.

TASK 6. A long sentence looks like it requires more time and effort to read. This alone can be off putting. So, if you are tempted to use commas throughout your sentence, don't. Instead turn your commas into full stops.

<u>Before</u>: Don't be kept waiting, take a number to ensure that you are served in turn and late comers do not jump the queue.
<u>After</u>: Don't be kept waiting. Take a number to ensure that you are served in turn and late comers do not jump the queue.

<u>Now you try</u>.
1. Watch this space for the latest specials on offer but do not delay, limits apply and shoppers must be quick to secure a saving.

_____

_____

_____

_____

_____

Change a long sentence into shorter ones.

You are not changing any words. You are just breaking your sentence into snippets of info.

2. This car park closes at midnight, any car locked in will incur an extra charge of $35 on top of the fee owed.

_____

_____

_____

_____

_____

3. Preheat the oven to 180 degrees, scoop the mixture into a greased muffin tray and bake for 40 minutes, then allow to cool before serving.

_____

_____

_____

_____

_____

Keep to one point per line.

This is the best way to cut down a long sentence into shorter ones without changing words.

4. Always re-read your emails before you send to look for typos and other errors, spell check does not apply to your outbox.

---

5. Ensure you switch off cruise control when you exit the highway, this way you will not risk driving above the speed limit.

Divide and conquer.

If any sentence has more than 21 words, just break it up. A few shorter statements will help to keep your readers focused.

6. Do not refreeze food, as soon as something defrosts it should be cooked, or you can store this thawing food in the fridge for a short time before using.

_____

_____

_____

_____

_____

7. If you do not have an alarm, call the front desk, a free wake-up call can be arranged for any time you wish day or night.

_____

_____

_____

_____

_____

Soon it will be second nature.
Get into the habit of turning commas into full stops.

8. Don't forget Daylight Saving will take effect in the early hours of the morning, best put your clock forward one hour before you go to bed.

_____

_____

_____

_____

_____

9. Replace the printer cartridge, then dispose of the empty one in the green bin, so it can be re-used rather than become landfill.

_____

_____

_____

_____

_____

**Don't forget, no more than
21 words a sentence, ever!**

10. Lodge your request three weeks before the day you want work to commence, this way any issues can be sorted without delays to your schedule.

_____
_____
_____
_____
_____

11. Make sure you fulfil each order by packing the right stock in the correct amounts, then send this to the address listed on the form.

_____
_____
_____
_____
_____

(Some answers listed at the back of this book)

LESSON 7
They don't say "brief" for nothing.

**"When you wish to instruct, be brief,
that men's minds take in quickly what you say,
learn its lesson, and retain it faithfully."
Marcus Tullius Cicero. Roman philosopher.
106BC-43BC.**

In the last chapter we discussed the value of concise writing. There are many times when succinct writing is the best way to go and never more so than when you are teaching. It should come as no surprise then that the word "brief" means both "instruct" and "to the point".

Life is full of lessons. Some are formal classes but, more times than not, we learn through other people sharing their knowledge with us.

For as long as there has been language, pearls of wisdom have been passed down. Perhaps these gems began as stories shared around a camp fire. Over time, though, these yarns have been dwindled down or cut to form those morsels of insight we call "proverbs".

These simple truths, based on common sense, have been compiled from many countries and varied cultures. Yet despite having a wide range of sources, proverbs comply with the one/two approach.

"Too many cooks spoil the broth."

"Empty vessels make the most sound."

"Those who live in glass houses shouldn't throw stones."

"There's no use crying over spilt milk."

"A stitch in time saves nine."

Are you seeing the pattern?

Sure, I admit it, listing five proverbs hardly amounts to research. So I delved further. In fact, I looked at over 500 sayings[xviii]. Even I did not realise that this many proverbs exist. Still, whether it was five or 500, the findings were much the same.

Of the 510 proverbs I used for my study, 419 (or 82 per cent) were solely made up of one and two syllable words.

When I looked at each word, though, the results were startling.

These 510 proverbs had a total word count of 3,614. Yet only 120 of these words had three or more syllables. Very simply, nearly all words used in these proverbs (97 per cent) were one or two syllables.

These proverbs also get straight to the point with the mean being just six words per saying.

Proverbs carry a lot of weight but they don't need length nor volume. So if wisdom, truth and morals can be conveyed in the simplest language, then surely it's the same for other learning.

If you need to instruct then simplest said is best.

All too often the "How To Guides" that are meant to assist us just leave us confused and bemused. Why? There are a number of reasons.

1.) More times than not, these booklets use complex terms, even jargon. If you need to instruct a first timer, speak in their language not yours.

2.) When experts write they tend to add more detail than is needed. Sure there may be times with this is called for but not when you are trying to instruct a novice. If you are teaching someone how to do something, only tell them what they need to know and nothing more.

3.) You might be able to multi task. After all you know your subject. But don't expect others to be able to handle many facets at the same time. If someone is new to the topic you're talking about, make just one point and let them absorb this. Only when they have grasped that step should you move onto the next.

So use simple language. Only tell your readers what they need to know. Also make just one point at a time. Do all these and each sentence should be easy for your readers to take in and apply.

Just look at The Ten Commandments.

This list of life rules forms the basis for many creeds. As the Bible tells it, "God inscribed two stone tablets that he gave to Moses on Mount Sinai". So if you believe that these are the work of a supreme being, you would expect them to be well written.

Of course, over the years, many people have had input, adding their touches to either the Exodus 20:1-17 or Deuteronomy 5:4-21 versions.

While these two do differ on some points they share much common ground. Each has ten sayings (or matters) that mostly comprise words of one and two syllables (vowel sounds)[xix].

In fact in Exodus it is 33:1. That is 33 words of one or two syllables for each word of three or more. For Deuteronomy, it is 26:1.

The Catholic/Lutheran version, by Augustine around 400AD, is the simplest of all Ten Commandments. Here there are 38 words of one and two syllables for each word of three or more. More to the point, in this condensed version, only two of the Commandments have a word of three syllables or more.

Even so, this is not what I want you to focus on here.

Up until now we have looked at what makes text simple. This time, though, let's take something simple and see if it is really improved by making it more complex.

For instance: "I am the Lord your God: you shall not have strange Gods before me". That's Augustine's version of the first Commandment. So let's change "strange Gods" to "extraneous deity". Now would that be a better choice of words?

How about "Keep holy the Lord's Day". Would it be improved if rather than "keep holy" we said "sanctify"?

Then there is: "Honour your father and your mother". How about we make that "continually uphold parental deference"? Then again, how about we don't?

"You shall not kill." Sure you could say: "You are forbidden from perpetrating homicide" but why would you?

Okay "you shall not bear false witness against your neighbour" may not seem very clear. Don't forget that this was written 1,612 years ago. So some words may seem a little odd by today's standards. If you changed "bear false witness" to "say anything mendacious", though, would that be any clearer? Yet often obscure words, like "mendacious" are used, knowing full well that most readers will have no idea what it means.

It's true. Some people would see a list, like The Ten Commandments, as their chance to wow us with their grasp of language. Hence my use of "mendacious" rather than the plainer "untrue".

So why do people feel compelled to over-write?

Throughout my career I've noticed that people resort to complex writing when they want their message to seem profound. Big words and long-winded statements are also used when the writer is supposed to be an expert. In fact, verbose and obscure writing is often wrongly believed to convey power, knowledge, class and level of schooling achieved. Even to promote a more costly product or service.

But why?

Your message is strong? You know your stuff? You have the very best product or service there is? Then why confuse the reader with a load of useless detail and cryptic wording? Instead let your message speak for itself - simply, clearly and briefly.

Never forget that if you really have something to say, just tell it the way it is. After all, it's your content that carries all the weight not the words you choose to use.

This time you may add, edit or change some words.

Aim for 21 words or less always.

TASK 7. Take each lengthy sentence below and turn it into two or more shorter ones. This time, though, you may have to make changes. Add, delete or alter any words as required.

<u>Before</u>: Read these papers from start to finish, answer all questions, then once complete, check and sign before placing in the envelope, sealing and posting.

<u>After</u>: Read these papers from start to finish and answer all questions. Then check and sign, before posting.

1. It's true that missing meals is not the way to diet because when we go hungry we risk binge eating the wrong foods.

_____
_____
_____
_____
_____

Turn each lengthy sentence into two or more shorter ones. If need be, you can remove, add or change words.

2. Wear gloves and a mask when handling this solvent and if you spill any on your skin wash in cold water straight away to prevent burns.

_____

_____

_____

_____

_____

3. During summer, because of the crowds, you must book ahead to reserve a table as we cannot hope to seat people who just walk in off the street.

_____

_____

_____

_____

_____

**Change each lengthy sentence into shorter ones
even if that means a rewrite.**

4. No-one may park in a lower ground car space without a green permit, signed and stamped by head office, then displayed on their windshield.

_____

_____

_____

_____

_____

5. When baking this cake, milk can be replaced by orange juice, oil can be used instead of butter and you can opt for the sweetness of honey if you would prefer not to add sugar.

_____

_____

_____

_____

_____

At first you will need to go back over your work to edit. But, with practice, you will become skilled at writing a concise sentence.

6. From 9am to 5pm weekdays, all calls will be charged at a peak rate, so to reduce your costs try to keep much of your phone usage outside of these times.

_____

_____

_____

_____

_____

7. If you wish to take time off you will need to complete an annual leave form, that you can get from HR, fill in the days you are planning to take and then return it to be approved.

_____

_____

_____

_____

_____

Have the hang of this now?
Let's do a last one for good measure.

8. Only staff who have been trained and assessed are able to use the workshop machines and they must comply with the list of safeguards displayed next to the switchboard.

_____
_____
_____
_____
_____

(Some answers listed at the back of this book)

LESSON 8
It's always about you.

"The most valuable of all talents is that of never using two words when one will do."
Thomas Jefferson - USA President who helped pen the United States Declaration of Independence.
1743-1826.

What's the subject you like most? You know, the topic that makes you stop in your tracks and listen. That one thing you never ever tire of talking about or reading.

Well you may not like to admit this. You may not even know it. But that topic is "you". And you are not alone there.

Whether we realise it or not, we all love to talk, hear and read about ourselves. So no matter what your subject, always try to present it from the reader's point of view.

In other words, rather than choosing "I" and "we", use the word "you" in your writing.

Some years ago, I started adding the word "you" to my ad copy. I started adding "you" to my direct mail letters and emails. I even started using the word "you" more in my chats with others.

In fact, these days, it's all about you as far as I am concerned and with good reason.

**Using "you" makes it clear who needs
to read, listen or take notice.**

We read so much in our day to day lives and most of it concerns others more than ourselves. So if you are writing to inform, advise or share then make sure the reader knows that this message is for them.

It's a no brainer but it needs to be said. The use of the word "you" is by far the simplest way to get a reader to take notice. And that's just for starters.

**The use of the word "you"
will also keep them reading.**

Of course, it is not a new concept. Ad land has long produced copy that conveys the "what's in it for you". In other words, even though these ads are selling products, it's not just about the brand. But rather what the brand's features do for the end user. How they help, save, support, comfort, delight, make easy or simply improve your lot.

So if you are writing something to promote a product or service, try and present it in the second person.

"You" may even boost response.

Some DM writers have gone so far as to claim this is true. That the response rate will indeed rise with the number of times the word "you" appears in the copy.

To be honest, though, I cannot see how you could research this. With a test, the idea is to change just one thing. This way you can be sure if that one thing worked or not.

But if you replace all mentions of "I", "we" and "us" with the word "you", the changes won't stop there.

When you use the word "you", it impacts the whole tone of the message. As such you would not just be changing one word but many. In fact, you could end up with a whole new sentence.

Even so, I would suggest that you put in more mentions of "you", even if that does mean a major rewrite.

After years of crafting direct mail and getting very good response rates, using "you" has worked well for me.

Plus, using "you" will make your writing appear less self-centred.

Some writers believe that using "I' rather than "we" makes their message warmer, from one person to the other. In fact, it's one of the first things I was told to do when writing DM letters. Now, looking back, I can see it has shortfalls.

Sure, when writing something you can change "we" to "I". Even so, you are still speaking in the first person. But by just adding the word "you", though, something truly special happens. All of a sudden the brand is thinking about the buyer. The student is thinking about the tutor. The boss is thinking about a staff member. The writer is thinking about the reader.

As such, your choice of the word "you" may not just make the reader sit up and take notice. It could even make the reader like you more than they did before.

This brings me to the next point.
Try not to repeat the same word
twice in a sentence.

A sentence becomes really boring if you repeat yourself. This does not just apply to the message but also your choice of words.

I can vaguely recall reading somewhere that the English language has the largest vocab. Not sure if that is true but one thing's for certain, we have more than enough words from which to choose. So, there's no need to repeat the same one even if you are keeping to words of one and two syllables.

For instance, try to avoid saying "and" twice in the same sentence. Instead you can use, "as well as", "along with" or "plus", to name some choices that you have.

But what's that, haven't I just broken this very rule in the last sentence? Yes, I have and with good reason.

While I suggest you don't repeat words, this does not apply to the word "you". Instead, I would advise you to use "you" as often as you can.

Never forget, there is real power in the word "you" so feel free to exploit it for all it's worth.

Look to add "you" as often as you can.

Write from the reader's point of view.

TASK 8 Pretend that the reader is a staff member, one of your target market, or just the person who will receive this message. Then write each sentence for them.

Of course, you will need to include the word "you" as often as required. But that is not all. Once you include the word "you", you may also need to rewrite the whole sentence.

<u>Before</u>: We are changing the system to make the whole process much faster and cost-saving for all concerned.

<u>After</u>: The system is being changed to make the whole process much faster and cost-saving for you.

Now try the next ones for yourself.

**Don't forget, use the word "you"
in each sentence below.**

1. We are sending out our new invoice. It has been designed to clearly show all charges and where any discounts have been applied.

_____
_____
_____
_____
_____

2. Our late model cars are being recalled to check the locking device. We will be taking bookings at all our service centres to ensure same day drop off and pick up.

_____
_____
_____
_____
_____

(Some answers listed at the back of this book)

Not "I" or "we" but "you".

3. For that next special event, we have a huge range of party items to buy and hire.

_____

_____

_____

_____

_____

4. The office will not open until noon on Friday to allow for building works to be finished in the entrance and foyer.

_____

_____

_____

_____

_____

(Some answers listed at the back of this book)

Write from the reader's point of view by using "you".

5. A comment box has been placed in the kitchen for staff feedback. This will be emptied at the end of each week.

_____

_____

_____

_____

_____

6. All staff should report to admin to collect their new password. This should then be changed to eight digits of their choosing.

_____

_____

_____

_____

_____

(Some answers listed at the back of this book)

Adding "you" will get others to read your writing. It's true.

7. Ensure that all books are returned by the due date or a late fee will need to be paid.

_____

_____

_____

_____

_____

8. This is not a self-seating café. Guests should wait at Front of House where they will be shown to their tables.

_____

_____

_____

_____

_____

(Some answers listed at the back of this book)

One last sentence.
Add "you" and, all of a sudden, your message
means much more to the reader.

9. If any shoppers are not happy with their purchase, they can return it within seven days for a full refund.

_____

_____

_____

_____

_____

(Some answers listed at the back of this book)

LESSON 9
Now let's recap.

**"Vigorous writing is concise.
A sentence should contain no unnecessary words, a paragraph no unnecessary sentences, for the same reason that a drawing should have no unnecessary lines and a machine no unnecessary parts."
William Strunk & E.B. White
"The Elements of Style". (1918).**

Does over-writing give us credence?

Will using cryptic language make our message more profound?

Would lengthy, heavy text get our readers to sit up and take notice?

Having worked your way through this guide I hope you answered "no" to each of these questions. Because as you should now realise, churning out verbose text requires very little thought and even less effort. What is more, this style of writing hardly makes for an easy read.

**It is quite a challenge to write
in a concise and clear way.**

After a lifetime of being programmed to use big words and long-winded phrases, this has become second nature. Hence this guide and the need to change mind sets.

"How to write an easy read" bridges a divide in large firms. Very simply, it helps execs write memos that staff in the plant, the warehouse and the stores can read with ease. It also ensures that those in the public read what you write and get the message. Even so, the tips inside this guide can be applied to other forms of writing.

If you want others to read, retain and even respond to what you write - then this guide will assist.

I strictly adhered to each of my easy read rules when writing this book. So if I can write over 17,000 words and stick to these tips, I'm sure you can work within these guidelines too.

So let's looks at the key points we have covered and see how they can go on serving you.

Keep most words to one and two syllables.

The best way to write simply is to use words of one and two syllables (or vowel sounds). Apart from proper nouns, of course.

With this guide we needed to break a lifetime of bad writing habits. It had to change a long-held belief that complex writing is the way to go. For this reason this guide went to extremes.

As you will recall, with the tasks, you were only able to use words of one and two syllables. Of course, in your daily life, there will be times when you must use a word of three syllables or more. Just as I found with "syllables", there are some words that cannot be said any other way.

For this reason you should aim for most words to be one or two syllables. Though, also realise that sometimes you have to use a bigger one.

As you have now become used to using smaller words, I would start with the aim of 63:1. That is 63 words of one and two syllables to each word of three or more. This is roughly a three or more syllable word in every third sentence. Given slogans, proverbs and even The Ten Commandments, 63 to one should be easy to achieve.

Of course, if this doesn't work, you can lower it later. But at least start by trying to meet the 63:1 target. After all, if there are too many big words you will no longer have an easy read.

When you must use a bigger word, spell it out.

At the start of the guide, when I used the word "syllable", I explained its meaning. I wrote "syllable (or vowel sound)". The same for paragraph (block of text). If you have no choice but to use a big word, always spell out the meaning in the simplest, clearest way.

This also applies to some proper nouns. If, in your workplace, you have a machine that has a rather complex name, then explain which machine you mean.

For instance, "To the left of the bed you will find the Defibrillator. This yellow device has leads, which connect to two pads, to help start a patient's heart".

No sentence should have more than 21 words.

A few smaller words are better than one really big one. The same applies to having a few shorter statements, rather than one lengthy sentence.

Commas are the culprit here. All too often we just keep adding to the one sentence until our statement covers many lines. When a sentence is too long, it looks harder to read. Why? Because it is harder to read.

Apart from "you", try not to repeat a word twice in any sentence.

In the last chapter we discussed using the word "you" as often as you can. And you should. But this only applies to the word "you". As for all other words, you really are spoilt for choice with the English vocab. So avoid saying the same word twice in any one sentence and your writing will seem fresh.

Convey just one point per line.

All too often you need to go back over a long sentence and re-read it. Even then it can make no sense, simply because too many points are being made at the same time. So follow how proverbs have been written, even The Ten Commandments and make just one point per sentence.

By aiming for a single message sentence, your writing will be much clearer.

Never have more than a six-sentenced para.

If something looks heavy, your readers can be put off even before they start. For this reason each paragraph (or block of text) should be contained.

Think small morsels of easy-to-digest info, rather than an all-you-can-eat buffet that will make your readers ill.

Don't forget that ease implies speed and vice versa.

If something looks like it will be quick, we assume it will be easy. For this reason, make sure your writing has lots of space around it. Short words, brief lines, contained paras all help create a page that looks easy to read.

**This brings me to my last tip
(one I haven't mentioned before).**

When writing, don't be afraid to have break out statements - such as a three word line, here and there. "It gets noticed.". "Why?" "Work it out."

You can also have a sentence that sits alone.

"Like this one."

A kind of para within itself.

So along with the words you choose and the ones you lose, the way your writing is structured also matters.

Don't forget that the more space you create, the better your message will stand out.

**What should you do if there isn't a smaller word
you can use?**

Reduce to its simplest form.

TASK 9. While you should always aim to make your writing concise, sometimes you must use words of three syllables or more. If this is the case, try to abbreviate (cut down) where you can.

For instance: Television is reduced to TV

OR Telephone is cut down to phone.

Now you try:
1. personal computer _____

2. refrigerator _____

3. university graduate _____

4. petroleum _____

5. kilograms _____

6. microphone _____

7. mineral turpentine _____

8. specifications _____

9. aggressive   _____

10. methylated spirits _____

11. resuscitate   _____

12. superannuation   _____

13. for example   _____

14. Compact disc   _____

15. etcetera   _____

16. temporary staff   _____

17. lubricant   _____

18. demonstration   _____

19. typographical error_____

20. taxation   _____

21. linoleum   _____

22. information technology_____

23. differentiator   _____

24. audio visual gear _____

25. administration _____

26. quotation _____

27. mathematics _____

28. laboratory _____

29. examination _____

30. identification _____

31. ammunition _____

32. introduction _____

33. limousine _____

34. rehabilitation _____

35. vegetables _____

36. vocabulary _____

37. sales representative _____

38. veterinarian _____

39. general practitioner _____

40. utility truck _____

41. saxophone _____

42. intelligence quotient _____

43. memorandum _____

44. maximum _____

45. legitimate _____

46. application _____

47. abdominal muscles _____

48. eyeglasses _____

49. revolutions _____

50. high fidelity _____
(Some answers listed at the back of this book)

LESSON 10
One last thing.

"Words, like glasses, obscure everything they do not make clear. Before using a fine word, make a place for it."
Joseph Joubert. French moralist and essayist. 1754-1824.

As you will now realise, it is quite a challenge to write an easy read. Even after you have mastered this skill, it will still require more effort than it does to churn out a whole lot of waffle. So, as we move forward, always allow yourself more time to perfect your writing into something clear and succinct.

This guide may seem quite short and to the point. But, believe me, each line has been crafted.

Throughout I've been careful to use words of one and two syllables (vowel sounds).

Each sentence is 21 words or less.

I have tried to avoid using the same word twice in a sentence. That's apart from the word "you" of course.

The paragraphs (blocks of text) are also contained.

Further to all these, no space has been wasted. Each lesson had to add value or it would have been cut from the mix.

This doesn't only apply to me though. You have to be just as mindful whether you are writing a report or a one-page office memo.

You have come a long way.
But this is still a work in progress.

For this reason, once you have tried your hand out there with your new-found skills, I suggest a refresh. Don't forget, these lessons can be done over and again. In fact, any time you need to remind yourself of the basics just do a task or two.

Once you start writing this new way on a daily basis, I also want you to take notice. In your line of work, field of study or way of life, there are sure to be words that defy being cut down. Terms you must use.

In these cases it is okay to use words of three or more syllables. But, to be sure that your reader does get the gist, always give more info.

This could involve having to explain what this term means. What this thing looks like. Or where it is found.

If there is ever any doubt, spell it out. In fact, this brings me to your tenth task.

At the end you will find a place to list those words you need to use that cannot be shortened.

Write those words in the back of this guide and describe each in simple terms. Then keep this on hand and refer to it each time you must use this jargon.

Most of all, though, don't forget that writing an easy read is a case of practice makes perfect. So take this new found skill and further improve it over time.

**What if a big word you must use
cannot be cut down?**

Spell it out.

Task 10A. If a word of three syllables or more must be used in full, then make sure you explain its meaning.

For instance:
Syllable (vowel sound).
Paragraph (block of text).
Abbreviate (cut the word to its simplest form.)

Dictionary   _____

Air conditioner   _____

Photocopier   _____

Ingredients   _____

Escalator   _____

Temperature   _____

Marketing   _____
(Some answers at the end of this book)

HOMEWORK

In your line of work, field of study or way of life, there are sure to be words that defy being cut down.

Make a list of these words below, and then describe each word's meaning. Now you can simply keep this list to refer to in future.

TASK 10B. List the hardest words.

Word _____ Explained as:

_____

Word _____ Explained as:

_____

Word _____ Explained as:

_____

Word _____ Explained as:

_____

Word _____ Explained as:

_____

Word _____ Explained as:

_____

Word _____ Explained as:

_____

Word _____ Explained as:

_____

Word _____ Explained as:

_____

Word _____ Explained as:

_____

Word _____ Explained as:

_____

Word _____ Explained as:

_____

Word _____ Explained as:

_____

ANSWERS

The list below is by no means complete. Instead it is just a sample of answers. So if at any time, you struggle, just refer to this list to kick-start your thinking.

TASK 1A - Employment: 1. Work. 2. Earning an income. 3. How you make a living. 4. Working and earning. 5. Job. 6. Paid work. 7. Being in the work force. 8. Line of work. 9. Charging for your work. 10. Being paid for your skills and talents.

TASK 1B - Education: 1. Schooling. 2. Formal learning. 3. Being taught how to do something. 4. Going to class. 6 To study something. 7. Being enrolled to learn. 8. Gaining knowledge. 9. Learning from experts in their fields. 10. Hitting the books.

TASK 1C - Malfunctioned: 1. Stopped working. 2. Faulted. 3. Broken down. 4. An error has occurred. 5. Is running badly. 6. Is playing up. 7. Is on the blink. 8. Has a problem. 9. Something wrong with it. 10. Is no longer in good working order.

TASK 1D - Obsolete: 1. Old fashioned. 2. Out dated. 3. Past its prime. 4. Not up to the minute. 4. Due for an upgrade. 5. An older style or model. 6. Time to trade up to something newer. 7. Not recent. 8. Ready to be retired. 9. No longer state of the art. 10. Ready for the scrap heap.

TASK 1E - Abbreviate: 1. Cut down. 2. Reduce words to letters. 3. Shorten. 4. Edit. 5. Abridge. 6. Expressed in the quickest way. 7. Use fewer words. 8. Make smaller. 9. Make it smaller and/or shorter. 10. Reduce.

TASK 2A - Calculations: 1. The math. 2. Number crunching. 3. Figures. 4. Do the sums. 5. How the numbers add up. 6. After taking all the figures into account. 7. After working through the numbers. 8. Reaching the total. 9. After adding some things and taking away others. 10. Counting it all up.

TASK 2E - Depreciation: 1. Reduced value since purchase. 2. Falling in value over time. 3. Worth less than its purchase price. 4. No longer worth as much as it was. 5. Dropping in value. 6. Resale price would now be reduced. 7. Sell it now and you'll get less than you paid for it. 8. Reduced resale value. 9. Not worth what it used to be. 10. How much it has fallen in value since it was purchased.

TASK 2I - Dissension: 1. Rifts. 2. Unrest in the ranks. 3. People not getting along. 4. Feuds. 5. Discord. 6. Disputes. 7. Conflict. 8. People upset with each other. 9. People not working well with each other. 10. People at odds with each other.

TASK 3 - Quick word changes. A. thanks. B. working. C. surveys. D. kept going. E. person. F. easy. G. entered. H. on their own. I. covers. J. notice. K. problems. L. highlight. M. sometimes. N. freely. O. task. P. somewhere to stay. Q. for being careful with money. R.

the same. S. better than the rest. T. constant watch. U. vital. V. press. W. give us a run through of. X. secured. Y. strike. Z. work out.

TASK 4 - Sentence **changes**. 1. Once all details are complete we can proceed. 2. Submit entries in writing. 3. Staff must clock in and out. 4. Admin has made some changes. 5. We have a program to welcome new staff and show them how things are done. 6. Here is how you can invest. 7. As those topics are not a key focus, we will not discuss them today. 8. Passing the exam is a must. 9. Some people have trouble grasping this. 10. There are plenty of ways to boost takings. 11. Being bossy is not good for team work. 12. All those using machines need to stay focused. 13. This role calls for good people skills. 14. We are looking for someone who is smart, well-spoken and bubbly. 15. When you apply please provide copies of all your papers. 16. This would only happen in extreme cases. 17. Please think before you answer. 18. Talks have commenced with all sections. 19. The stock has been listed and warehoused. 20. We expect that the piece will have a local feel. 21. It is vital that you work with each other on this project. 22. It all comes down to how you see things. 23. That person can be too forthright with others. 24. Make sure you know the new laws then put them into action.

TASK 5 - Cut it out. 1. really, all. 2. extra, this unit. 3. only. 4. helpful. 5. watchful. 6. good, with you. 7. surely help to, some of the. 8. ensure, you, always. 9. the right amount of, very well, whole. 10. safely secured or safely under lock and key. 11. be, sharp. 12. twelve times a year or monthly. 13. all the way through. 14. To you, the very. 15. total or all up. 16. many and varied, on the best one for you. 17. very much, and parcel. 18. rather than pretend, you with your query. 19. make a point to, keep this on. 20. from start to finish, with the others. 21. scheduled, all, at length. 22. will, under the building. 23. faulty, constant, all kinds of. 24. sale, greatly, 50 per cent, so you can buy it for. 25. single, one after the other, your name, it.

TASK 6 - Turn commas into full stops. 1. Watch this space for the latest specials on offer but do not delay. Limits apply and shoppers must be quick to secure a saving. OR Watch this space for the latest specials on offer. But do not delay. Limits apply and shoppers must be quick to secure a saving. 2. This car park closes at midnight. Any car locked in will incur an extra charge of $35 on top of the fee owed. 3. Preheat the oven to 180 degrees, scoop the mixture into a greased muffin tray and bake for 40 minutes. Then allow to cool before serving. OR Preheat the oven to 180 degrees. Scoop the mixture into a greased muffin tray and bake for 40 minutes. Then allow to cool before serving. 4. Always re-read your emails before you send to look for typos and other errors. Spell check does not apply to your outbox. 5. Ensure you switch off cruise control when you exit the highway. This way you will not risk driving about the speed limit. 6. Do no refreeze food. As soon as something defrosts it should be cooked. Or you can store this thawing food in the fridge for a short time before using. 7. If you do not have an alarm call the front desk. A free wake-up call can be arranged for any time you wish day or night. 8. Don't forget Daylight Saving will take effect in the early hours of the morning. Best put your clock forward one hour before you go to bed. OR Don't forget. Daylight Saving will take effect in the early hours of the morning. Best put your clock forward one hour before you go to bed. 9. Replace the printer cartridge. Then dispose of the empty one in the green bin so it can be re-used rather than become landfill. 10. Lodge your request three weeks before the day you want work to commence. This way any issues can be sorted without delays to your schedule. 11. Make sure you fulfil each order by packing the right stock in the correct amounts. Then send this to the address listed on the form.

TASK 7 - Aim **for 21 words or less always**. 1. It's true. Missing meals is not the best way to diet. When we go hungry we risk binge eating the wrong foods. 2. Wear gloves and a mask when handling this solvent. If you spill any on your skin, wash in cold water straight away to prevent burns. 3. During summer, you must book ahead to reserve a table. Because of the crowds, we cannot hope to seat people who just walk in off the street. 4. No one may park in a lower ground car space without a green permit, signed and stamped by head office. Please make sure this is displayed on the windshield. 5. When baking this cake, milk can be replaced by orange juice and butter can be used instead of oil. You can also opt for the sweetness of honey if you would prefer not to add sugar. 6. From 9am to 5pm weekdays, all calls will be charged at a peak rate. To reduce your costs, try to keep much of your phone usage outside of these times.

7. If you wish to take time off you will need to complete an annual leave form from HR. Fill in the days you are planning to take and then return it to be approved. 8. Only staff who have been trained and assessed are able to use the workshop machines. They must also comply with all the safeguards listed next to the switchboard.

TASK 8 – Write from the reader's point of view. 1. You will soon receive our new invoice. It has been designed to clearly show you all charges and where any discounts have been applied. 2. Your late model car is being recalled to check the locking device. You can simply book in at any of our service centres to ensure same day drop off and pick up. 3. If you have a special event, you can pick and choose from our huge range of party items to buy or hire. 4. You should not arrive at the office until noon on Friday as building works are being finished in the entrance and foyer. 5. A comment box has been placed in the kitchen for your feedback. This will be emptied at the end of each week. 6. You should report to admin to collect your new password and then change this to eight digits of your choosing. 7. Ensure that you return books by the due date or you will need to pay a late fee. 8. This is not a self-seating café. Please wait at Front of House so we can show you to your table. 9. If you are not happy with your purchase, you can simply return it within seven days for a full refund.

TASK 9 - Reduce to the simplest form. 1. PC. 2. fridge. 3. uni grad. 4. petrol. 5. kilos. 6. mic. 7. turps. 8. specs. 9. aggro. 10. metho. 11. do CPR. 12. super. 13. eg. 14. CD. 15. etc. 16. temp. 17. lube. 18. demo. 19.

typo. 20. tax. 21. lino. 22. IT. 23. diff. 24. AV gear. 25. admin. 26. quote. 27. math. 28. lab. 29. exam. 30. ID. 31. ammo. 32. intro. 33. limo. 34. rehab. 35. veggies. 36. vocab. 37. sales rep. 38. vet. 39. GP. 40. ute. 41. sax. 42. IQ. 43. memo. 44. max. 45. legit. 46. app. 47. abs. 48. glasses. 49. revs. 50. hi fi.

TASK 10. Spell it out. Dictionary - a book of words and their meanings. Air conditioner - a machine that cools the air. Photocopier - a unit that copies papers. Ingredients - all the foodstuffs that are used to create a meal. Escalator - stairs that are powered to take people up one flight. Temperature - how hot something is. Marketing - pushing a product or service.

READINGS AND SOURCES

To arrive at the findings in this book, many quotes, speeches, slogans and proverbs needed to be reviewed. These were gathered from a range of sources, listed below, then assessed purely for their structure. The content was neither here nor there. Instead the research involved counting the proper nouns, words, syllables, as well as how many points were made per sentence, among others. Only then could comment be made.

[i] Daniel M. Oppenheimer gave permission for his findings to be referred to in "How to Write an Easy Read" 8 November, 2011.

[ii] William Shakespeare "The Complete Works of William Shakespeare Hamlet Prince of Denmark" Act 3 Scene 2 Page 1092 published by Crown Publishers, Inc.

[iii] Whitlam Speeches: 1972 'It's Time' Policy Speech (http://whitlamdismissal.com/speeches/72-11-13_ it's=time.shtml), 13 November, 1972. Retrieved 23 March, 2012.

[iv] Shamshullah, Ardel (December 1992). "Australian Political Chronicle: January-June 1992: Victoria". *Australian Journal of Politics and History* 38 (3): 426-427. ISSN 0004-9522 (http://www.worldcat. org/issn/0004-9522). Retrieved 23 March, 2012.

[v] http://en.wikipedia.org/wiki/New_Labour,_New_Life_For_Britain. Retrieved 23 March, 2012.

[vi] http://en.wikipedia.org/wiki/Things_Can_Only_Get_Better_ (D: Ream_song). Retrieved 23 March, 2012.

[vii] http://en.wikipedia.org/wiki/Barack_Obama_presidential_campaign_2008. Retrieved 23 March, 2012.

[viii] https://en.wikipedia.org/wiki/George_W._Bush_presidential_campaign,_2004. Retrieved 23 March, 2012.

[ix] http://www.presidentsusa.net/campaignslogans.html. Retrieved 19 December, 2011.

[x] For the purpose of assessing this address in terms of the number of words, proper nouns, syllables and so forth, the source used was: http://avalon.law.yale.edu/19th_century/gettyb.asp. Retrieved 5 December, 2011.

[xi] For the purpose of assessing this speech in terms of the number of words, proper nouns, syllables and so forth, the source used was: http://old.news.yahoo.com/s/ynews/ynews_p1135. Retrieved 6 December, 2011.

[xii] http://www.guardian.co.uk/world/1940/jun/18/france.thefarright. Retrieved 5 December, 2011.

[xiii] In order to assess a fictional work the number of words, proper nouns, syllables and so forth, the source used was: Harper Lee 1960 "To Kill a Mockingbird" Chapter 1, page 3 published by Arrow Books. The Random House Group Ltd.

[xiv] In order to assess a fictional work the number of words, proper nouns, syllables and so forth, the source used was: J.D. Salinger 1951 "The Catcher in the Rye" Chapter 1, page 5 published by Penguin Books

[xv] In order to assess a fictional work the number of words, proper nouns, syllables and so forth, the source used was: William Shakespeare "The Tempest" printed 1964 Act 1 Scene 1 page 37 published by The New American Library.

[xvi] In order to assess a fictional work the number of words, proper nouns, syllables and so forth, the source used was: William Shakespeare "The tragedy of Romeo and Juliet" printed 1964 Act 1 Scene 1 page 42 published by The New American Library.

[xvii] In order to assess slogans in terms of the number of words, proper nouns, syllables and so forth, the sources used were: http://www.nowsell.com/marketing-guide/list-of-advertising-slogans.html. Retrieved 3 January, 2012. http://www.adglitz.com/2010/08/24top-n-best-100-ad-slogans-taglines-punchlines-advertising-campaigns. Retrieved 3 January, 2012.

[xviii] In order to assess proverbs in terms of the number of words, proper nouns, syllables and so forth, the source used was: http://www.phrases.org.uk/meanings/proverbs.html. Retrieved 7 February, 2012.

[xix] In order to assess The Ten Commandments in terms of the number of words, syllables and so forth, the source used was: http:en.wikipedia.org/wiki/Ten_Commandments.